Teddy Bears of the Rich and Famous

by Mark Leigh & Barney Leigh

Based on an original idea by Mike Lepine & Mark Leigh

Published by Accent Press 2010

ISBN 9781907016363

Printed and bound in Hong Kong

Design by Neil Michael Lodge

Introduction

Sigmund Freud, in his little-known theory, 'The Teddy Bear and Subconscious Post-Natal Development' (Vienna, 1923), hypothesised that far from being just an adorable, cuddly and comforting companion, teddy bears have a great influence on the development of our formative years – shaping our personalities and even professions. Contemporary critics described this theory as ludicrous, absurd or 'scheisse' however modern psychoanalysts have seen sense and meaning in Freud's findings, collating evidence that he was, indeed, correct.

This book is a collection of these examples; teddy bears dressed and accessorised by their young, innocent owners which, history has shown, clearly established their adult characters and career paths.

Illustrations include the teddy bears of people as diverse as the Queen, Damien Hirst, David Beckham, Leonardo Da Vinci, Madonna, Picasso, Simon Cowell and even Freud himself. See for yourself how their childhood toys have shaped their futures and enjoy, Teddy Bears Of The Rich & Famous.

Mark Leigh & Barney Leigh
Surrey, England 2010

Borat's bear

3

Darth Vader's bear

Leonardo da Vinci's bear

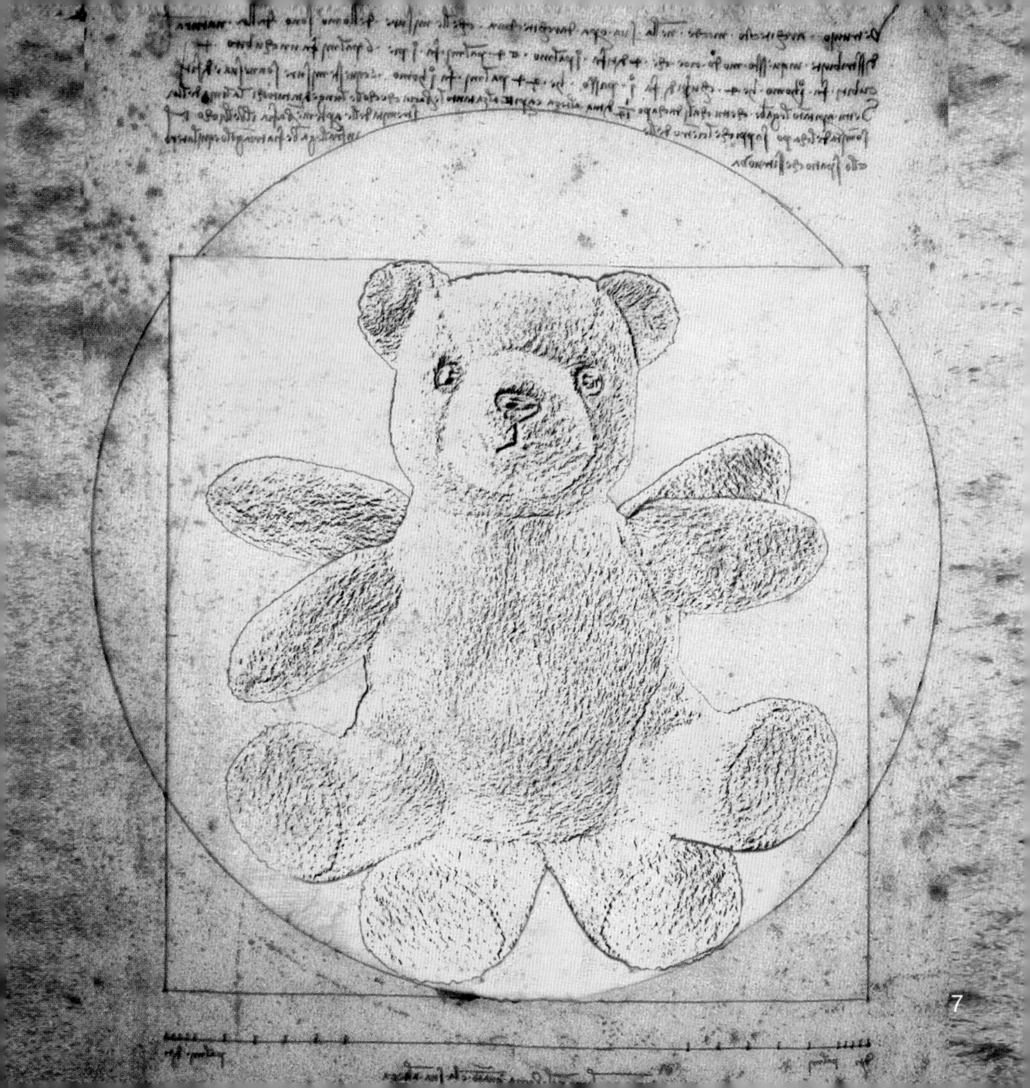

David Beckham's bear

Steven Spielberg's bear

PAWS

11

Van Gogh's bear

David Bowie's bear

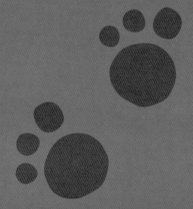

Banksy's bear

William Tell's bear

19

Che Guevara's bear

21

Madonna's bear

Damien Hirst's bear

A A Milne's bear

Albert Einstein's bear

29

Andy Warhol's bear

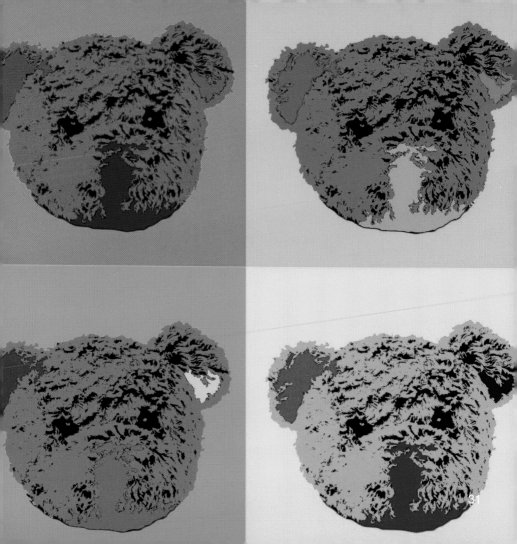
31

Cleopatra's bear

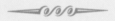

33

Christine Keeler's bear

Arnold Schwarzenegger's bear

—∽∼∿∽—

Dame Edna Everage's bear

39

Bob Marley's bear

41

Captain Jack Sparrow's bear

Adam's bear

Neil Armstrong's bear

Hugh Hefner's bear

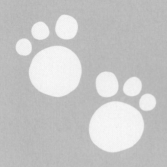

Early Man's bear

Florence Nightingale's bear

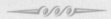

Johnny Rotten's bear

Audrey Hepburn's bear

Hannibal Lecter's bear

59

Kevin Spacey's bear

BIG TED
7 3 3 4 1 1

9"

8"

7"

6"

61

Mary Shelley's bear

Stanley Kubrick's bear

Michael Jackson's bear

—ↄɷↄ—

Bill Gates's bear

Dr Seuss's bear

71

Mr T's bear

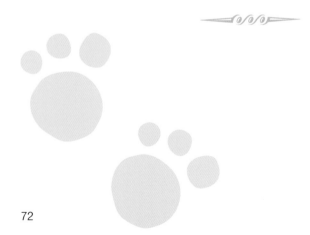

Pontius Pilate's bear

King Henry VIII's bear

Roy Lichtenstein's bear

The Queen's bear

Paul Daniels's bear

Sigmund Freud's bear

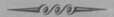

Victoria Beckham's bear

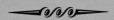

Tutankhamun's bear

Simon Cowell's bear

Houdini's bear

Thank you

The authors would like to thank the following people for their kind assistance and input:*

Darin Jewell, Debbie Leigh, Polly Leigh, Adam & Sarah Sherman, Ian Turnbull, Sara Howell, Miriam, Hope & Miles Markham.

*Between you and me, most of their ideas were absolutely ridiculous and we had to humour them but there were one or two suggestions that were fairly sensible.

MEET THE AUTHORS

Mark Leigh

Is the author / co-author of 38 published humour & trivia books including the best selling How To Be A Complete Bastard & Pets With Tourettes and is currently working on a novel and movie screenplay. Mark lives in Surrey with his family & his teddy bear, Siegfried, who's he owned since the age of two. When not writing he works in advertising and relaxes by playing bass in his Death Metal Band, 'Blunt Force Trauma'.
www.mark-leigh.com

Barney Leigh

Is currently studying for his A Levels at Esher College, Surrey. With a creative bias to his course, he enjoys Vocational Media and English Language and one day aspires to have a career in film directing/editing. Barney's other passion is music, and he regularly enjoys waiting outside venues in a bid to catch/stalk the musicians. The artists he is currently most proud of meeting are La Roux and The Drums. In his spare time, Barney enjoys trying not to turn into his father.
www.barneysfascinations.tumblr.com